WOLVERHAMPTON
MADONNA

✦

WOLVERHAMPTON MADONNA

✦

Jeff Phelps

OFFA'S PRESS

2016

First published in 2016 by Offa's Press,
Ferndale, Pant, Oswestry, Shropshire, SY10 9QD.

ISBN: 978-0-9955225-0-3

Typeset in Baskerville Old Face
Designed by Marie Jones, printed and bound
by Lion FPG Limited,
Oldbury Road, West Bromwich, B70 9DQ.

CONTENTS

Inventing Mother in London

after Lynn Emanuel – *Inventing Father in Las Vegas*

If I could see nothing but the smoke
from her Kensitas I would know everything
about that trip to the Palladium.
If her lips were dark with Elizabeth Arden I would know
this was a street in Kensal Rise,
a hotel room with a sign over the pavement,
her nylons across the back of a chair,
the restaurants grey and navy with uniforms.
I could be the glamour of that meal
she shared with her Polish airman.
I would be the rush of air at her kissed mouth
in the underground at Piccadilly.
If I could become the trumpeter busking the queue
in the West End, the pavement would be slick with bus light
and she would put a penny in my hand.
I would read the programme through her eyes,
fold it and use the opera glasses
from the seat in the gods, squeezing his hand
for fear of falling.
If I could be the choice she made
whether to stay with him or return
I would say *Go, go,*
uninvent myself in the process.

Cooking in a Bedsitter
Katharine Whitehorn, Penguin, 1970 edition

You talked me through my first shy fumblings
with white bread dipped in egg then fried.
French toast you called it.
You always were a slice above the rest of us,
your seasoned words making Cordon Bleu
of our daily eggy bread.
Cooking in a bedsit was ever thus,
the Baby Belling with its single ring,
the thin, aluminium saucepan.
You turned me, Katharine,
from gauche milksop to assured student,
showed me the gradual, patient foreplay
of flour and milk,
the fulminating miracle of Béchamel sauce.
Then, you and I were as easy with Chicken á la king
as scrambled egg on toast.
Oh, how that toast still scorches in my heart.
Everything I know
about long grain and basmati
I learned from you.
Alas, it's all behind us now.
We both moved on, as we knew we must.
I have an oven, fan-assisted, a microwave,
and meals so instantaneous
it would have made you weep.
Yet, Katharine, we share much more than memories.
The other day I came across our paperback.
It opened in my hand,
pages loose as lasagne leaves,
that chicken curry recipe we loved so much
still brown with spattered ghee.

Triolets

I

We don't have to talk about love.
Why don't you phone me? Please.
Any subject will do – hearing you would be enough.
We don't have to talk about love.
We could discuss plays and poetry or any of that stuff
and get more personal by degrees.
We don't have to talk about love.
Why don't you phone me? Please.

II

Forgive me if I haven't said
how much I like you. I know it's a kind of lying
not to say things but keep them hostage in my head.
Forgive me if I haven't said
what I think you want to hear. It's just saying it I dread.
Your eyes, reproachful, would be worse than dying.
Forgive me if I haven't said
how much I like you. I know it's a kind of lying.

In the Blood

I always thought our family was staunchly loyal:
Alec at D-Day blowing German tanks apart,
Dad with the Signals on Belgian soil.
These were the adventures I knew by heart
and only later learned of great uncle Bill –
Welsh Socialist and conchie to the end
who campaigned with Keir Hardy and wouldn't kill
some German boy who might have been his friend.
When the Redcaps came Gran hid him double quick
in the coal shed, bit her chapel tongue and told a lie.
Still he spent his war in Cardiff nick,
chopped wood beneath a chilly English sky.
I remember him much later – old and lean,
sitting in Gran's parlour. There was shame
unmentioned like a dormant family gene
that might emerge in one of us again.
Courage comes in many forms for sure
and I was never called so I don't know
but I suspect I would have gone to war
like all those brave lads, terrified to go.
But uncle Bill, obeying a different call,
risked rifles, blindfold against a wall.

First Boyfriend

Your boyfriend bought you flowers –
Glyn, you said was his name –
two bunches, one of roses
and one of yellow tulips,
both wrapped in supermarket cellophane.

The label on the tulips said
'Guaranteed to last at least five days'
and I remembered what you'd told me:
'One day I'll get flowers from a boy.'
Not that long ago. A prophetic turn of phrase.

He texted you three times a night
and phoned you in between.
You said it was flattering,
yet somehow oppressive, and anyway
he kissed like a washing machine.

I admired the way you knew what you wanted
even at your age – those budding, intuitive powers.
Yet I still felt kind of sorry for your boyfriend;
kissed and dumped within a fortnight,
he lasted hardly longer than his flowers.

Note of caution for a son going off to university

Of midnight encounters with the law,
of pubs that lock the inner door,
of too much detergent in the washing machine drawer
be careful.

Of women who say 'I'll call you back',
of botulism, Little Chef, Big Mac,
of dandruff, pyorrhoea, plaque,
be careful.

Of the condom borrowed from a well-meaning friend,
of accelerating into an unlit bend,
of staying at the party till the bitter end,
please, *be careful.*

When mixing metaphors, mixing drinks,
avenging pranks, creating stinks,
studying all night or unblocking sinks,
at least try to *be careful.*

Of being self-righteous, intolerant of vice,
of being impatient, of being too 'nice',
and regarding poems spiked with advice,
son, *be careful.*

Wenlock Edge

At night, when you were homesick,
your brother told you to look up
and think of us at home,
continents away, watching the same
shared moon.

This field closens us, too.
When you come back I'll show you
how it tilts up to The Edge,
how wind, soughing through bands of ash and hazel,
marks that boundary, like falling into space.
Today, a sky lark hangs, rising and rising.
Its fluttering song fills the basin of the air.

Ice once clunked and ground its way here,
sliced through hills, thawed to a broth.
Now every stone turned over at the field edge
carries the memory of warm seas:
coral, stone lily and shattered ammonite.
The earth ploughs itself endlessly,
churns up its treasures.
It settles and moves,
understands no boundaries, secretly
brings us together.

Oxygen

Halfway up the climb we stop
to catch our breath.
Hearts, thumping and pumping
have outgrown cages
and want to be away.
Sun and oxygen make us dizzy.

From here valleys are folded
in origami new perspectives;
villages come clear of trees
and ridges link from violet to pink and haze.

And, Dad, I am with friends I know you'll never meet.
At a thousand metres I think of you
there at sea level,
mask pressed over mouth and nose
like some desperate fighter pilot.
The tired, leaking bellow of your lungs
half fills, can't hold long enough.

How sharp the air is up here
and plentiful, yet still we gasp and grasp for it;
thermals lift us with the buzzards.
We climb on as if to deny some deadly gravity.

But you, mainlining oxygen,
are bound to earth by plastic tubes,
grounded by iron cylinders.
In your living room you adjust the valve
and catch a breath,
snatch another minute's worth of air.

Wine Glasses
In memoriam Seamus Heaney

Wine glasses must be washed first
in water hot as hands can bear, untainted
by the everyday of cutlery and plates.
Rub out the deep red lees, invert them,
stems-up to stand like potters' kilns.

I think I had forgotten what a poem was
till you reminded me how the world can be made
to scintillate on a single wavelength.

Now I hold the glass up to the light.
The taut brittle arc of its bowl is faith
in the impossible. I rub a moist finger round the rim,
hear a kind of gathering, a resonance that's neither
glass nor air, but a new place between.
Its high sound fills the kitchen like a prayer bell.

Madonna and Child

Painting by Marianne Stokes known as
the 'Wolverhampton Madonna'.

You might have seen her in Queen Square
or standing opposite Beatties with her child,
just a babe in arms, asked
how did she afford that blood-red cloak,
the dark velvet lapels?
A charity shop? Some soft-hearted passer-by?
You will have recognised the appealing tilt of her head.
It makes you feel bad just for being there,
makes you want to cross the road.
Her baby is wrapped in crepe bandage, of all things,
and what looks like a net curtain. Another charity job.
Both have those fine-boned East European features
and such eyes, Aegean blue. Not accusing exactly and not proud,
more resigned, asking nothing but questioning everything.
You can see it on the streets any day,
the way some mothers use their babies for sympathy
to squeeze a quid out of you.
Her hand slips from the warmth,
lifts to show his face, but all you think is:
he could do with warm milk inside him.
You'll have seen her outside the train station,
by the magistrates' court
or sometimes, as this evening,
waiting on a patch of waste ground
before golden brambles
some loose angelica,
a harvest moon for halo.

Marianne Stokes (1855-1927) was an Austrian artist who travelled and
painted extensively in Europe. Madonna and Child *was painted in Dubrovnik in*
1905 and was modelled on a local girl from the city. It is currently in
Wolverhampton Art Gallery.

Art Teacher

Didn't want to think of you
trying the coffin for size, or planning
the colour schemes yourself
when you were still alive.
Didn't want to imagine
your loved ones mixing pigment,
practical concerns about its longevity,
the paint's reaction with the burners.
Far better to have you
painting your own way in, mad
as Jackson Pollock with a spray gun,
or else those Lautrec limbs you so admired
carting you away on a circus horse,
La Goulue whipping up a storm
of green and white and indigo.
For company you would have that *Déjeuner sur l'herbe*,
the blue of snow in the lee of fences,
a thumb pot by your thumb
and, wound in your whiskers, a bristle brush
to paint your way home.
Now you can describe an arc like Blake's
that burns through the earth,
up past Turner's rain and steam and speed,
to break out finally
into the blaze of afternoon light you told us about
that still rattles the underside of leaves
and stirs the bathers at Asnières.

Wells

The chapter house is placid as a pond.
One slender column spurts and overspreads,
spatters into rib and lily frond,
cascades over alcoves with sculpted heads
of long-gone clergy; ugly, ordinary men
whose voices bubble to the surface, rise and dip.
It is these stairs that beckon them again:
like the way to heaven, treads eroded to a lip
by seven hundred years of heels before us.
Waters meet at a curving brimming weir.
If stones could sing and light was the chorus
these stairs are what we would hear -
prayer pouring from the chapter house tower
sluicing down into every cloistered hour.

After the Deluge

Ducks are in the birdhouse
where the robin used to sit.
They're eating from the bread bin
which is floating next to it.

Eels are in the meter cupboard
getting electric shocks.
Water voles are reproducing
in the letter box.

There's a heron in the kitchen
where the blender used to be
and he's dipping in the fridge for
frozen kippers for his tea.

Rice grows in the rockery,
the drive is full of trout,
and even plastic gnomes are pulling
seven pounders out.

You have to see the funny side
and have a little grin –
with all our downstairs upstairs
and all the outside in,

I never really knew that
there was so much life out there;
but now I watch it floating past
from the comfort of my chair.

Goose Girls

They call from a childhood I never owned –
two barefoot girls on the river island.
Stumbling over rocks
they stoop to pick up feathers
and thread them in their hair,
heavy as curling papers,
strong as goose wings.
They look up and wave,
hoot with laughter.
Then they are gone.
There is only white litter in the stones,
geese battling the stream,
two in flight.
I hear the gentle gust
of air and beak-blow,
the rattle of wing beats
and I am left on the parapet like Daedalus,
begging them to fly close,
to be careful,
to stay wild.

River Map

You can read this river like a map.
These arrow-shaped ripples, an acute accent,
are where there was a ford. Even today
you can cross carefully at low water
like Jesus and hardly damp your feet.
The stillness, that glassy pool
was once deep enough for wherries and trows to moor.
The marks of the wheel are visible,
the rub of the rope if you know how to look.
You can hear echoes in the stone.
You can read this map like a river,
trace fingers where brooks and pale springs rise
from Potseething to Dowles, surging
out of forests,
past mills, laundries and forges,
a blue Braille of history
leaving names behind
like silt.

River Passage

In the classroom
old Beddow punches dots on the board
with a snap of chalk-end, a crumbling of dust on the wood block floor.
He punctuates the word
eye-sos-alees
with dots for emphasis
and on the third drills the board
with finger nails to make the class wince.
At least some signs of humanity, he thinks –
make them show they are alive.

Outside it rains.
Mizzle. Fine Clee Hill rain
lining up on the fascia
like school kids. Dot to dot,
blown before its time onto the window
which mists and thaws and runnels
into lines, not parallel,
but merging, beyond the logic
of any geometry.

Dave is in the school yard –
left last year as soon as he could
after exams, but still feels a distant
sense of belonging. He rides a mountain bike
with ten Shimano gears,
understands poetry as a hand
untangling rabbits from the ferret net,
the taut, frightened look of a leveret.
And now he cycles emptily
through dry and wet and dry,
under the shelter, through patchy puddles,
half seeing tyre lines
merge and separate on the tarmac,
half hearing the zizz of water on rubber,

the screek of brake blocks in the wet,
thinks passingly of a job driving Massey Combines
and has already forgotten Beddow's lessons,
their fading, sad symmetries.

Dave is too early for his younger brother,
who sits at the back of Beddow's class,
too early for the bell,
only halfway through maths,
the lesson's dozing nadir.
Passing across the yard
the young PE man tells him to clear off,
to go to the Job Centre if he has nothing better
and Dave registers blue tracksuit, new Reeboks,
not suited to the damp,
the rising of moisture like up a drain.

He skids his bike as he retreats,
sassily outside the gym, standing on the pedals,
the shimmy of rear wheel not unlike
the distant tail-wag of a Spitfire
over Tern Hill or Stanmore
signalling to those on the ground
its safe return.

In boredom more than anger
Dave lobs a block of rubber down the bank
forgetting the road is there below.
The block arcs, a low but perfect parabola
to land in nests of dock, campion,
young unformed dandelion, harebell and blackberry,
a whole nation of wild flowers on the by-pass bank,
and rolls on squarely, bouncing
on to the road.

From his driver's seat
Jonathon sees the tumbling block first,

the kid second, in silhouette
at the bank top, turning handlebars
as if to escape.
Jonathon brakes but the rubber dings,
reverberates under the wheel arch
and flies behind and he breathes
'Bloody kids', watches in the mirror
as the rubber dances, takes life in the road,
rolls and comes to rest in the gutter.
Driving over the by-pass bridge
Jonathon glimpses a hump of a town,
piled on a cliff and copper-topped;
looks at the river which is spring-height,
glistening like a snail-trail,
punctuated with green umbrellas
like cabbages.

Upstream is a tree
where cormorants, black as dead leaves sit,
circle, then dip for fish. On damp days like these
they are a mirage, fish stealers,
returning to their tree to preen,
bills under oily feathers, learning to live
a hundred miles from home,
unwelcome as Black Country bikers on a Sunday.

Jonathon sits under his green sky,
the pattering canvas of a fishing umbrella,
watches the river spit drops
and casts his line upstream.
The silence, the concentration is what he loves,
the nylon angle, the dip of fluorescent float;
that and the strike,
the timing of which no maths can predict,
when the barbel closes its mouth
and comprehends, suddenly, a new element
with which it was always connected

in a perfect straight line.
You learn to avoid cormorants,
the scavenging incomers.
You wait instead for the electric blue
of kingfisher,
a drenching of moorhens,
a squabble of ducks.
Jonathon reels in
to let a canoeist pass,
to avoid lines becoming snagged.
They nod in mutual, resigned acceptance
of one another's right to be there
of their different perspectives of the river.

Richard dips the paddle,
heaves water behind him.
Helmet, canoe, lifejacket, spraydeck;
how many families of moorhens he has dispossessed,
water voles forced by his bow wave
into upper chambers.
He times the strokes like an Oxford cox,
thinks of his arms, his stomach muscles,
of the return trip, which will be harder –
the Jackfield rapids, the pubs, the bridges,
the caravan parks, all mopped up
by the swing and strike of one arm over the other,
the dip and dive as sure as an otter
that gives him the feel, the knowledge that,
eye-level with swans
he has a right to be here.
His glasses sweat with spray
as he trails one paddle;
a watery skid and the Bridgnorth bridge
comes into sight, buttresses
jammed with logs and the spring's drift.
Beyond the bridge
Richard pulls in to clear his vision.

Impossible in such a wet place;
nothing to wipe spectacles on.
He clutches an overhanging branch of hawthorn
and breathes on a lens.

Suddenly he is swept round by the current,
feels the stern go and the glasses slip through his fingers
He reaches for them, tries to catch,
like catching fish with your hands.
They bounce on his fingertips, slip from the deck
and he has reached too far.
He always goes too far, he thinks,
as he topples, loses it. With a shoulder
he smacks green water, breathes filthy bubbles.
Now upside down, Richard thinks he sees the glasses
shimmer up through floating green galaxies,
like spots you get before your eyes,
dislocated particles of retina.
He could almost touch them even now,
but for the different geometry of underwater
where there's no time to breathe,
where everything moves
in slow motion.
Richard remembers the drill;
is surprised that, even here,
instinct snaps into place. He tries
to paddle himself upright
but something traps him,
is stronger than paddles,
than the desperate torque of shoulder muscles –
he recognises it as the clutch of a branch or, worse,
the unexpected, concentric gravity
of a whirlpool.

One night, two years ago,
a lad went in upstream from here.

The river has the body now, never found,
the town riddled with underwater mazes,
carved sandstone gullies
with entrances, no exits,
two hundred miles of water keeping him in place,
feeling his pockets for identity,
searching the hair.
The boy lives under water,
bone love to the sandstone,
all the money out of his pockets,
credit cards gone, washed away.
He crouches under a thousand years of sandstone
like a foetus in decaying denim,
stone washed by the river.

Before he turns
Richard, inverted, afraid to breathe,
looks him in the eye.
Then he is righted, paddles, splashes,
gasps. He never knew how precious air could be.
What he would have given for air, then.
Green water slides off the deck
and he opens his eyes
as if for the first time ever,
to reeds and willows and smell of water,
the sound of traffic on the by-pass
and the sun, water sliding past it.

Richard persuades himself
this encounter was an aberration,
a desperate imagination playing tricks.
But for old Beddow the splash the boy made
still thumps in his ears two years later.
It was he who heard it that night
as he walked Meg, his springer.
The dog stopped at the sound.

This is how he described it to his wife
afterwards, trembling a little,
unable to drink the brandy,
and the dog asleep in front of the gas fire.
It's how he remembers it still,
wishing he could have done something,
but knowing it had slipped,
the moment, through his fingers.
He told a policewoman the same –
a splash, some distance away,
heavy like a bag of potatoes
then nothing. Nothing.

Sometimes in the night he wakes even now
thinking he has heard it, or else the echo of it.
Or it's the lights of the police helicopter
he has dreamed of, sweeping the river;
how he stood and watched
while Meg sniffed for rabbits,
as it kept coming back
to where water rippled darkly.
You could have drawn a line between the places it stopped,
as if there was some connection between the spots of light.

Now old Beddow joins dots with a new chalk
chosen from the blackboard trough
as if white on black will make them understand
this ancient Greek mapping –
still as true today as then.
A thought of helicopters crosses his mind
fleetingly as a dragonfly on a river.
Old Beddow, feeling a chill from the open window,
puts on his jacket,
blows chalk dust from his sleeve.

Roadside Trees

(i)

How many years?
It must be twenty or more
we have driven past
on the journey to relatives,
the road threading its way round
so at first the tree's in front,
then off to the right,
perfect as an exhibit
wrapped in swathes of lawn.
It stands oblivious to our visits
through seasons,
so perfectly an oak,
and always there is the same detail -
from a low branch
a tyre hanging from a rope.
I have never seen anybody on it.
I always said I'd photograph the tree,
but hedges and those curves
allow nowhere to stop.
It slides past us every time
unreeling, like childhood,
into the countryside.

(ii)

The skid points it out -
a broken sixty mile an hour arc on the road.
Leaves unfurl above, as if nothing had happened,
but the trunk is gashed bare,
an exclamation of tree flesh
at waist height.

It ends in a litter of faded colour -
pots of dahlias from the local florist,
daffodils turned brown,
cellophaned sheaves of chrysanthemums
and, caught between reticence and love,
those card votives,
hastily penned notes to the children
whose short journey ended here.

(iii)

Two sycamores
stand on the roadside,
each trunk marked
with a clear white cross
and above,
neatly painted,
a capital letter F.
They stand like truants
outside the headmaster's office,
like tarred and feathered collaborators
in the market square.
We avert our eyes,
almost embarrassed
by such a public fall from grace.
We are the ones not stigmatised.
We may choose other interpretations,
pretending not to understand,
but in our hearts we know
nothing good will ever come
to any helpless being
marked with F.

Swallows

No curves can describe the trail they blaze
through summer evening air.
Not figures of eight,
or scythings of letters Z or S.
Not even tangled Sanskrit or pictogram
contain their fluid way.
They are linked by mewing blips.
They are water gurgling up through the sky.
They swerve,
avoiding easy definition,
through swarms of summer insects
feeding their way through dizzy atmospheres,
open throats constructing
mile-high dot-to-dot.

Blackberries

The day after you died
I picked blackberries.
It felt irreverent,
like robbing the grave of someone recently buried
and trivial
compared to the enormity of your death.
I should not be here I thought
and wondered which plump cell
it was that had altered your heart
and finally stopped it beating.
But there they were, the blackberries,
rich and dense as the whole perfect summer
clustered in fists for taking.
It was easy to fill the container
with sweet fruit and all different.
Some were past picking and wore
the cobweb sheen of autumn.
Some, overripe, fell to the ground
in pieces as I reached for them
or resisted the tug and stayed
safe among thorns.
Others were ready.
At hardly a touch they gave themselves,
gently dropping
into an open hand.

Spring Funeral

Frogs have occupied the shallows of the pond.
This first April sun has brought them out,
to squat under leaves,
their liquid eyes digesting light,
black throats quivering.

You should have been here, amongst friends
to see them. You would have showed us
how words can dissect
as exquisitely as blades,
assuring us that here is a renewal
we must go on sharing.

They seem to multiply.
By an optical trick there are more
each time we look:
khaki heads bubbling up,
two where we thought there was one.

You would know
they wouldn't let us touch them.
But still we try,
our hands outstretching slowly.
They slip away at the last moment,
flop sideways into deeper water,
leaving us in mid-gesture.

Angry Haiku

Haiku has no sense
of humour. Sitting there in
its samurai kit

it pontificates
about leaves and seasons and
drops hints about 'Life.'

Haiku never laughs.
Haiku never gets pissed or
falls down in the street,

never farts or needs
to borrow a quid. Never
uses words like 'bum'

or 'pontificate'
which bristles with syllables.
It's smug. Refuses

to say a single
word more than necessary;
a mealy-mouthed bint

which, if taken to
a disco would whine, 'Sorry,
I don't know this one.

I only do the
five-seven-five. Strict tempo.
I'm a little stiff.'

You argue. Haiku
refuses to be drawn. 'Christ!'
you shout, 'If only

you'd rhyme, do something
crazy.' You begin to wish
that you'd spent more time

in loose company,
fooling around with ballads,
tangling with free verse.

Too late. Haiku blinks,
stands up to dance, cold-fingers
the back of your neck.

Acknowledgements

Some of these poems were published in the following magazines: *Envoi, Headlock, Orbis, London Magazine, The Interpreter's House* and *The Rialto*.

Some were published in these anthologies: *We're All in This Together* and *The Poetry of Shropshire*, Offa's Press, *Reading Allowed*, Bridgnorth Writers' Group, and the Wenlock Poetry Festival anthologies. The poem *Wine Glasses* appears in the anthology *The Everyday Poet: Poems to Live By*, Michael O'Mara, 2016.

After the Deluge was broadcast on Radio Shropshire and included on the CD *Live at the Lych Gate*, Offa's Press. *Angry Haiku* was commended in the Manchester Open Poetry Competition, 1997.

River Passage was second prize winner in the Stand Open Poetry Competition, 2000, and published in *Stand*. It has also been published with illustrations by Jayne Gaze, 2002, and as a CD by Offa's Press with piano music by Dan Phelps, 2010.

Madonna and Child won second prize in the Bishops Castle 'Provocations' competition, 2012. *Inventing Mother in London* was second in the Wenlock Poetry Festival open competition, 2015, and published on the Wenlock Poetry Festival website.